The
Sacramento
River

The
Sacramento River

by OSCAR LEWIS

illustrated by Michael Hampshire

HOLT, RINEHART AND WINSTON

New York   Chicago   San Francisco

Contents

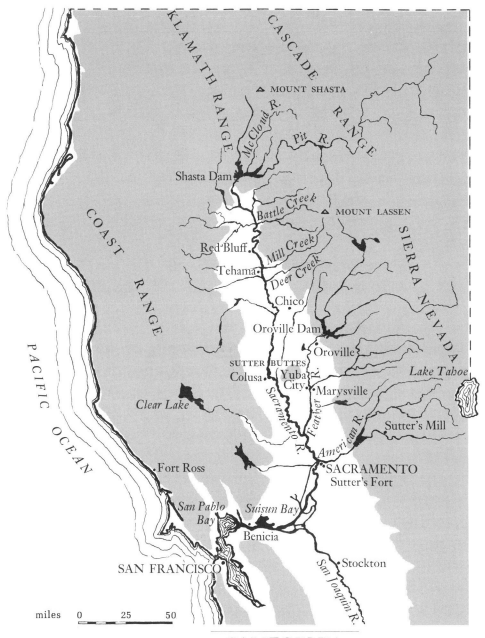

KLAMATH RANGE

CASCADE RANGE

△ MOUNT SHASTA

McCloud R.

Pit R.

Shasta Dam

Battle Creek

△ MOUNT LASSEN

Red Bluff

Mill Creek

SIERRA NEVADA

Tehama

Deer Creek

Chico

COAST RANGE

Oroville Dam

Oroville

SUTTER BUTTES

Colusa

Yuba City

Lake Tahoe

Sacramento R.

Feather R.

Marysville

Clear Lake

American R.

Sutter's Mill

PACIFIC OCEAN

Fort Ross

SACRAMENTO

Sutter's Fort

San Pablo Bay

Suisun Bay

Benicia

Stockton

SAN FRANCISCO

San Joaquin R.

miles 0 25 50

CALIFORNIA

1

The Setting

IN the typical central California landscape, as viewed from any commanding summit, the noble frankness of nature shows one at a glance the vast plan of the country.

THESE words by the noted philosopher Josiah Royce, who spent his childhood at the edge of California's Central Valley, help one picture the immense region drained by the Sacramento and San Joaquin rivers.

A glance at a map of California will make clear the outlines of what Royce called nature's "vast plan." For occupying the center of the state and extending more than two-thirds its length is a valley nearly six hundred miles long and from seventy-five to one hundred miles wide. The valley is ringed by mountains. Only on the west is there a break in the encircling wall. There, near the middle of the state's thousand-mile-long coastline, a cleft appears in the Coast Range. Through this gap the valley's two rivers flow into San Francisco Bay and thence through the Golden Gate into the Pacific.

1

This break divides the coastal mountains into two nearly equal parts. The northern section, which closely follows the coastline and in many places rises abruptly from the water's edge, is a series of ridges running north and south and separated by narrow, steep-sided valleys. A luxuriant growth of trees and shrubs blankets the hillsides from base to crest, and in the flatlands below stand great forests of the world's oldest and tallest trees, the majestic redwoods known to scientists as *Sequoia sempervirens*.

South of San Francisco Bay the valley's western wall curves inland. The forests of redwoods, oaks, and madrones gradually thin out, then disappear entirely, and the range becomes a succession of gently rounded hills. During the early spring, fields of poppies and wild lupine spread over their surfaces, forming bright tapestries of blue and gold and green. This brilliant display lasts only a few weeks; then the rainy season ends, and the flowers and grasses burn dry. Throughout the remainder of the year the hills are the color of straw, accented here and there by thin bands of green where thickets of live oaks and manzanita bushes trace the course of the streambeds.

Walling in the valley on its eastern side is the mighty Sierra Nevada, a quite different sort of mountain range. In terms of geology, the Sierra is much the younger of the two ranges. Whereas countless centuries of erosive action have reduced the once rugged coastal mountains to a series of smoothly outlined hills, in the Sierra nature's leveling process has hardly begun.

The lofty Sierra dominates the landscape from every part of the valley. In the foreground are the rolling foothills, their sun-bleached grasses shimmering in the heat of the long, dry summers. Beyond are the lower reaches of the mountains themselves, an intermediate series of ridges rising tier above tier and covered to their crests with forests of pine and spruce and cedar.

From these the eye is carried upward to the distant summit of the range. During the summer months heat rays rising from the valley's floor often obscure the view. But if the day chances to be clear, the wall of uptilted granite rises high above the forests, its snow-covered summit sharply outlined against the sky. This mass of granite is a slate gray, capped by fields of dazzling whiteness where the snowpacks on the higher peaks reflect the sun. From time to time thunderclouds gather and drift across the landscape, casting dark shadows on the faces of the cliffs.

The entire western side of the Sierra is a complex of deep ravines formed over the centuries by torrents of water coursing down from the melting snows above. In their swift descent to the lowlands some streams flow into mountain lakes; others continue down into the foothills, and having been joined by others, become tributaries of the Sacramento and San Joaquin.

At the southern end of the valley the two mountain ranges merge and form a third, the Tehachapis. The word is of Indian origin and means "frozen water," perhaps because ice forms each winter about the edges of its streams. Unlike the Sierra and the northern half of the Coast Range, which because they receive abundant rainfall are well forested, the Tehachapis support only a sparse growth of vegetation, chiefly sagebrush and gnarled piñon pines.

Standing guardian over the far northern end of the valley is

3

the massive bulk of Mount Shasta. Its 14,162-foot crest, perpetually mantled with snow, is visible for scores of miles in every direction. Over the years many have recorded their impressions of this towering landmark.

Joaquin Miller, the "Poet of the Sierras," who as a youth in the mid-1850's spent several years in the area, likened it to a spirit that, "white as a winter moon . . . starts up sudden and solitary from the heart of the great black forests of northern California." Another who wrote eloquently of Shasta was the naturalist John Muir, who described it as a "fire mountain" that had been "thrust upward into the deep blue of the sky by successive eruptions."

As John Muir's words imply, Mount Shasta, unlike the mountains of the Sierra and the Coast Range, is of volcanic origin. Its twin summits were once craters formed in prehistoric times by masses of molten rock forced up from below. After its ancient fires were quenched, long before the arrival of the white man, the mountain's surface was deeply furrowed by the thrusts and pressures of slow-moving glaciers during the ice age.

Slightly less than a hundred miles to the southeast of Shasta stands a somewhat lower peak, Mount Lassen. Lassen too is a "fire mountain," but unlike Shasta, it has remained intermittently active down to the present. The last time its crater stirred to life was in 1914, when over a period of several months a series of eruptions sent columns of smoke and steam and ashes high into the sky. The awesome displays then decreased in force and frequency and finally ceased entirely. Today Lassen is classified as a dormant volcano, although the many hot springs about its base are evidence of underground fires close to the surface.

It is in the southern half of the Sierra that the mountains that rim the valley reach their greatest height. From Lake Tahoe to the headwaters of the Kern River, a distance of more than two hundred miles, the range is a series of lofty ridges broken by mile-deep canyons down which course swift streams fed by the snowpacks above. On their passage to the lowlands these are joined by others. By the time they reach the valley floor they have become tributaries of the Sacramento and San Joaquin.

Midway in this area is the world-renowned Yosemite Valley, which Thomas Starr King, who camped on its parklike floor in the summer of 1860, termed "the grandest piece of rock and water scenery in the world." The Yosemite Valley was first glimpsed in 1833 by members of Joseph Reddeford Walker's pioneer trapping expedition. But it was not until 1851, when a party of soldiers under Major James D. Savage pursued a band of Indians into the valley, that the breathtaking beauty of lofty granite cliffs and mile-high waterfalls first became known to the world. Since then its wonders have been viewed by thousands of visitors each year.

To the north and south of Yosemite are a number of mountains that rise more than two miles above sea level. Highest of all is Mount Whitney. Named for Joseph D. Whitney, onetime chief of the California Geological Survey, the mountain has an elevation of 14,495 feet—the highest point in the United States outside of Alaska. Other summits in the area are only slightly lower. Yet, such is the rugged nature of the region that only a few miles to the southeast lies Death Valley, the floor of which at one point is two hundred feet below the level of the ocean, making it the lowest spot on the continent.

Life in California's Central Valley has been influenced in many ways by the wall of mountains that shuts it off from easy communication with its surroundings. One result of its centuries-long isolation is that certain varieties of trees, shrubs, and grasses are common there but rarely grow on the other side of the mountains. What is true today of the vegetation native to the valley once was also true of its animal life. We know from the accounts of early-day hunters and trappers that animals—notably the grizzly bear and the California cougar, or mountain lion—were numerous there, but virtually unknown beyond the mountains. Others, frequently met elsewhere in the west, were seldom seen in the valley.

The letters and journals of visitors to the Sacramento Valley during pioneer days rarely failed to mention its abundant wildlife. Some tell of flocks of ducks, geese, and other migratory birds so large that they darkened the sky for days on their flights to and from their winter feeding grounds. Others wrote of rivers and streams abounding in fish, of large colonies of beaver, otter, and other fur-bearing animals, and of immense herds of deer and elk grazing on the lush grass of the valley's floor.

The lives of the valley Indians were likewise influenced by their environment. Because of the encircling mountains, they had few contacts with the coastal tribes or those to the north or east and so developed customs and skills that differed from those of other western tribes.

Compared to that of other West Coast Indians, the natives of the valley lived a life of ease. The climate was mild and pleasant, without extremes of heat or cold. Whereas the tribes farther north were obliged to build shelters for protection against winter snows, the Indians of central California were able to live in the open the year around. The roofs and walls of their makeshift huts were made of reeds or brush or the skins of animals, the fronts of which were usually open to the weather.

Because there was an abundance of fish and game and ample supplies of acorns, pine nuts, and other favorite foods, the valley Indians were a friendly, peace-loving people. Until the coming of the white men the valley tribes lived in harmony with each other. Each tribe had its own hunting grounds, the boundaries of which were clearly defined. The foothill tribes usually occupied all the land drained by a single stream, their domain reaching to the crest of the hills on either side. Those on the valley floor occupied areas extending from the river-bank to the foothills and bordered on the north and south by streams flowing into the Sacramento River. It was only when one tribe trespassed on the hunting grounds of another that intertribal warfare broke out. And because it was rarely necessary for them to venture beyond their own territory in quest of food or other supplies, such clashes were infrequent.

It was only after the arrival, in the early 1840's, of the first large parties of emigrants from beyond the mountains that this situation changed. As the white men settled in the fertile valley, the natives were forced from their ancestral hunting grounds and fled into the foothills. The hill tribes opposed this intrusion from the lowlands, and when they sought to repel the invaders by force, a series of pitched battles resulted.

Thus the era of peaceful coexistence enjoyed by the Indians of central California for many generations drew to a close.

2

The Last of the Yanas

THE Indians who occupied the lands drained by the Sacramento River belonged to many different tribes and subtribes. Each was ruled by its own chief, each spoke its own language, and as we have seen, the members of each rarely strayed beyond the borders of their own hunting grounds.

The native population was divided into six major groups. The Wintuns, Maidus, and Miwoks occupied the floor of the valley from the Sacramento–San Joaquin delta to the base of Mount Shasta, a distance of two hundred miles. The territory of the Wintuns was west of the river, and that of the Maidus and Miwoks on the east. The other three were mountain tribes. The northernmost, the Chimarikos, lived in the heavily forested Klamath Range in the northwest corner of the present state of California. Adjoining them on the east was the Shastan tribe, after which Mount Shasta was named.

The third hill tribe was that of the Yanas, who occupied the rugged country north and east of the Sacramento Valley's northern end. A comparatively small tribe both in numbers

10

and in the size of their territory, the Yanas were surrounded by more powerful neighbors: the Wintuns to the west and the Shastans and Maidus to the north, east, and south.

The Yanas in turn were made up of four subtribes. We are concerned with the southernmost group, a people called the Yahi, who lived in an area of chaparral-covered foothills, rocky uplands, and toward its eastern boundary, dense forests of pine and fir and spruce. The region is traversed by two streams, Mill Creek and Deer Creek, which, fed by the snowfields of the Cascade Range to the east, flow down to the valley and eventually into the Sacramento.

Because they occupied a district that had few attractions to the white man, the Yanas were permitted to retain their lands long after the valley tribes had been dispossessed. The first white settlers all chose to establish their ranchos on the valley's floor, where ample fertile land was to be had for the asking and where the Sacramento River offered a convenient means of shipping cattle, grain, and other products to market. Several decades passed before the desirable valley land had all been put to use and the cattlemen began moving their herds into the foothills.

Thus, until the former Mexican province was ceded to the United States in 1848, and for some years thereafter, the Yanas lived much as they always had. Even the discovery of gold in January of that year, which drew thousands of miners into the foothills, brought few changes to this remote region. To be sure, from time to time parties of prospectors made their way up Deer and Mill creeks into the heart of the Yahi country. But few traces of gold were found there, and the

11

miners continued on to richer diggings in the newly opened Shasta-Trinity area, some eighty miles to the northwest.

By the mid-1850's, however, the yield of the placer mines had declined to the point where to many their operation was no longer profitable. The miners abandoned their claims and returned to the valley, took up land there, and became farmers. And as the large cattle ranches that had once covered the entire floor of the valley one by one were broken up and put under cultivation, the stockmen moved their cattle and sheep to new grazing grounds in the foothills—and the territory of the Yahis. In the face of that invasion from the lowlands, the Yahi tribesmen were forced to retreat ever farther into the heavily wooded back country.

They presently found themselves surrounded on all sides by white settlers, but because they were skilled woodsmen, and because they had intimate knowledge of their remote hide-away, they were able to avoid any contact with their neighbors. This despite the fact that the ranchers sometimes visited the area on hunting or fishing expeditions or while searching for stray animals. So completely did they conceal themselves that as years passed without one of their number having been sighted, the Yahis came to be regarded as an extinct tribe.

But unknown to the outer world, the remnants of the once numerous tribe had somehow managed to survive. During all that time their bows and arrows, spears, snares, and nets—all of which they fashioned themselves—had provided them with food and with the skins of animals from which their clothing, blankets, and the covering of their shelters were made.

Meanwhile their refuge had grown steadily smaller as more

and more of their land was taken over for summer grazing ranges by the stockmen. The time came when the small space remaining no longer provided them with sufficient food. Thereupon, driven by hunger, they began making stealthy raids on the outlying ranches and making off with a stray sheep, and on occasion breaking into and rifling a sheepherder's cabin.

For a time the ranchers were mystified by such raids. The culprits were never seen, and the articles taken—usually worn-out clothing, discarded cooking utensils, even bits of cloth or metal—seemingly were of no value to anyone. But as the unexplained thefts continued, and animals and other property disappeared, the suspicion grew that a mysterious band of "wild Indians" might be responsible.

That suspicion eventually turned to certainty. One day in

the spring of 1885, as a rancher approached an isolated cabin on upper Mill Creek, he saw several figures climbing from its window. Caught by surprise, the long-haired, dark-skinned strangers—an old man, two younger men, and a young woman —made no attempt to flee. Instead, they lined up before the cabin and waited, motionless and silent, while the rancher rode up. Because they had taken nothing of value, he made no attempt to detain them. After a few moments they turned and, still silent, filed off along the trail leading upstream.

Several months later the Mill Creek cabin was broken into again. This time nothing was taken; instead, two large grass baskets were left behind. It was assumed that the Indians had intended them as tokens of gratitude for the owner's lenient treatment of them during their earlier visit.

Following the surprise meeting at the cabin, the Yahis appear to have been careful to avoid other such encounters. In this they succeeded so well that, incredible as it seems, more than twenty years passed before there was another direct confrontation between the tribesmen and their white neighbors. Meanwhile, the occasional disappearance of a calf or sheep, or the rifling of a cabin, kept alive the belief that a mysterious band of "wild men" might be lurking somewhere in the heavily wooded back country. However, as time passed, such incidents became less frequent and finally ceased entirely. By the early 1900's the "wild men" theory had been all but forgotten.

Then, in the spring of 1908, a party of surveyors who were running a line down the canyon of Mill Creek stumbled on the well-concealed spot where the remnants of the tribe lived.

By then their number had been reduced to four: a mother, a son and daughter, and an elderly man. Three of the four had fled at the approach of the white men, but the mother was too old and ill to be moved. That night the son had stolen back and carried her into the hills, but she had died soon after. The other two had evidently met the same fate, for although the son had searched for days, he never saw either again.

Another three years passed. Then, early on the morning of August 31, 1911, near the town of Oroville, a former mining town in the Sierra foothills, the crew of a stockyard were awakened by the excited barking of dogs. On investigating the cause of the commotion, the workmen found a bedraggled figure crouching in a corner of the corral. The stranger had unkempt black hair, copper-colored skin, and black eyes, then wide with fear, set in a broad face. His thin body was unclothed except for a tattered blanket about his shoulders, and his posture was one of extreme weariness.

The county sheriff was notified, and the stranger was taken to the Oroville jail. There he remained for several days, making no reply to questions and evidently too terrified to eat or sleep. The town officials were at a loss to know what to do with their prisoner, who seemingly had appeared out of nowhere and about whom they could learn nothing.

While they pondered their problem, a message arrived from a member of the Department of Anthropology of the University of California at San Francisco, offering to take charge of the stranger and to be responsible for his welfare.

The offer, which was gratefully accepted, had been made by Professor T. T. Waterman, an anthropologist who had

15

made a study of the northern California Indians. On reading accounts of the "Oroville wild man," as the newspapers called him, Waterman had concluded that he might be a member of one of the hill tribes who had spent many years in hiding, until, driven by loneliness or hunger, he had wandered down to the lowlands. The spot where the stranger was found was less than fifty miles from the old hunting grounds of the Yanas.

During his first meetings with his protégé at the Oroville jail, Waterman put his theory to the test by reading lists of words from the dialects of three of the four subdivisions of the tribe. (No list had been made of the language of the fourth subtribe because at the time the lists were compiled the Yahis were believed to be extinct.)

While the professor went through his lists, pronouncing each word distinctly, his companion listened closely. For some time his face remained impassive; it was clear that the words meant nothing to him. Presently Waterman came to the word *siwini*, which in the southern Yana dialect means the wood of the pine tree. As he spoke he tapped the frame of the cot on which they sat. At once the uncomprehending look on the Indian's face vanished and his eyes lighted with pleasure. At last he had heard a familiar word!

The readings continued, and the now keenly interested listener soon recognized other words. At first progress was painfully slow, but a beginning had been made. The Yahi, delighted that someone could speak to him, however haltingly, in his own tongue, had shunted off his air of bewilderment. Soon he was cooperating eagerly, volunteering words of his own and correcting the pronunciation of his companion.

In preparation for the journey to San Francisco, where the Indian was to be housed at the Museum of Anthropology, Waterman persuaded his charge to put on the white man's clothing—all, that is, except shoes, which he found so uncomfortable that he refused to wear them.

To this child of nature, who had spent all his life—he was then about fifty years old—in the wilderness, the train ride down the Sacramento Valley, the ferry trip across San Francisco Bay, and the drive through the city streets, was literally a passage from one world to another. It was an ordeal that might well have confused and terrified the Yahi, yet he bore it with stoicism. Then and later he conducted himself with dignity, full of interest and curiosity about the wonders he saw on every side, yet giving no evidence that he was over-awed by them.

Because his mentors never learned their protégé's true name —or, indeed, if he had ever had one—they christened him Ishi, the word for "man" in the Yahi dialect.

Ishi spent the final five years of his life at the museum. He was assigned to quarters with the janitorial staff and quickly learned to sweep and dust and perform other simple tasks. As he became familiar with his surroundings and his familiarity with the language grew, he entered actively into his new life. Before many weeks had passed he had lost his reserve and was joining his new friends on sightseeing trips about the city, taking part in their games, and visiting them at their homes.

All the while scholars at the museum were gathering information about his former way of life. From Ishi they learned the story of the last years of his doomed tribe, how, cut off from their sources of food and other necessities, the struggle for survival had become ever more difficult. By the time the surveying party discovered their hideaway in 1908, the once numerous tribe had been reduced to four: Ishi himself, his mother and sister, and an elderly warrior. Little was ever learned of his experiences during the three years he had lived alone in the wilderness. That it had been a time of great hardship and privation may be inferred from the fact that Ishi rarely spoke of it. When it became clear that the subject held unhappy memories for him, his mentors refrained from asking further questions.

But of other aspects of his former life he spoke freely. From him much was learned of the day-by-day habits and customs

18

of California's primitive people. On several visits to his tribe's old hunting grounds he demonstrated the methods by which they had provided themselves with food and clothing and shelter. Using tools he himself had made, he fashioned bows and arrows, spears, snares, and other devices, all of superior workmanship, and showed how each was used. He also gave practical demonstrations of basket weaving, the preparation and cooking of food, the making of clothing and blankets from the skins of animals, and other handicrafts.

Throughout his stay at the museum, Ishi's helpfulness and unfailing good humor, and his pleasure at all he saw and heard, made him a general favorite. During most of his five years there he enjoyed good health. Toward the end of his stay, however, he fell victim to tuberculosis, a malady to which the California Indians were particularly susceptible. He died on March 25, 1916.

The stone that marks his grave bears this simple inscription: "Ishi, the last Yana Indian, 1916."

3

Trail Breakers

THE discovery of America ushered in a period of exploration that enormously expanded the frontiers of the known world. Within half a century after Columbus' first voyage the wide-ranging galleons of Spain, England, and other seafaring nations had rounded Cape Horn and made their way up the west coasts of both South and North America.

In the fall of 1542 two tiny vessels flying the flag of Spain and commanded by the Portuguese navigator Juan Rodríguez Cabrillo explored the coast of much of Alta California, charting the shoreline and conferring names on headlands, inlets, and other landmarks sighted along the way.

During the second half of the sixteenth century and the early years of the seventeenth, a number of other ships visited the remote far-western land. The *Golden Hind*, commanded by the English freebooter Francis Drake, arrived in 1579; Sebastián Cermeño's *San Agustín* followed in 1595; and in 1602 three small Spanish vessels, the *San Diego*, *Santo Tomás*, and *Tres Reyes*, put in at Monterey Bay, where their captain,

20

Sebastián Vizcaíno, laid claim to the country in the name of his sovereign, King Philip the Second.

Although from that time on the Spanish rulers considered California part of their New World empire, nearly two centuries passed before any attempt was made to take formal possession of the land. It was not until 1769 that the first permanent settlement was established there. That came about because other Old World powers were believed to be casting envious eyes at the potentially rich province, and it was deemed prudent to provide means of defending it against attempts to take it over by force.

The belated colonization of California followed a procedure Spain had used in its other New World possessions. It had three major purposes: that of making the colony safe from foreign aggression, of encouraging settlers to take up land there, and of Christianizing the natives and training them in the ways of civilization. To accomplish those ends a number of towns (*pueblos*), military posts (*presidios*), and missions— the latter presided over by priests of the Franciscan order— were founded along the coast from San Diego northward to San Francisco bay and beyond.

Of the three types of settlements, it was the missions that wielded the most influence throughout the early period. Beginning with the founding of the first mission in 1769, their number grew rapidly, until by the early 1820's they totaled twenty-one, spaced a day's travel apart and extending two-thirds the length of the present state. During their most active period they sheltered close to thirty thousand natives, who, under the direction of the padres, built a series of imposing

churches and other buildings (some of which still stand); cultivated the mission fields, orchards, and vineyards; manned the shops and workrooms; and tended large herds of livestock.

Nearly all the Spanish settlements occupied the narrow strip of land that lies between the ocean and the mountains that parallel the shore. Of the interior of the province almost nothing was known. To be sure, groups of soldiers or civilians sometimes pursued bands of natives beyond the mountains to recover horses or cattle stolen from the mission herds or those of the *rancheros*. But such forays rarely penetrated far inland; consequently, little was learned of the Central Valley as a whole.

The formal exploration of the region drained by the Sacramento and San Joaquin rivers began in 1811. The first expedition to the Sacramento was led by Sergeant José Antonio Sánchez. With a party of sixty-eight men he left the San Francisco presidio in mid-October. Traveling in open boats, they made their way through the Carquinez Strait into Suisun Bay, and after spending several days searching through the maze of sloughs and estuaries of the Sacramento–San Joaquin delta, located and entered the channel of the Sacramento. By then, however, the party had run short of provisions, and after rowing a short distance upstream, they turned about and returned to their starting place.

In the spring of 1817 Lieutenant Luís Argüello, the *comandante* of the presidio at San Francisco, led a party of soldiers and native oarsmen on a second exploratory mission to the Sacramento Valley. Argüello and his crew traveled aboard a launch, the *Santa Rafaela*. Accompanying them was a second craft, the *San José*, in the charge of two missionaries, Fathers Ramón Abella and Narciso Durán. The record of their journey is preserved in a diary kept by Father Durán. In it he tells how, after a difficult voyage up the bay, during which their open boats were buffeted by strong head winds, they entered the delta, and after another long search, located the mouth of the river. For seven days they pushed upstream. The broad, placid river, bordered on both sides by tall cottonwoods and offering vistas of oak-strewn plains beyond, so aroused Durán's admiration that he likened the country to a "king's park."

Although the smoke of distant campfires was sighted from time to time, of the natives themselves nothing was seen. Daily the party encountered great herds of deer, elk, and other animals, and at the approach of the boats immense flocks of wild-fowl rose from the water and circled overhead. Father Durán reported, too, that the river abounded in fish.

Three years later, in 1821, Lieutenant Argüello again led a party up the Sacramento; this time he planned to follow the stream all the way to its source. Although the expedition fell far short of that goal, it was the first to penetrate into the heart of the valley. Like Father Durán before him, Argüello made a record of his voyage; his was in the form of a map on which he traced the course of the river and conferred names on some of its tributaries. The northernmost stream shown on the map is the Feather River, which empties into the Sacramento at a point some thirty miles above the present city of Sacramento. Because of many feathers floating on its surface, Argüello christened it Río de las Plumas.

The next white men to explore the valley came by land. These were the far-ranging "mountainmen," a hearty breed of hunters and trappers who, beginning in the mid-1820's, had been breaking new trails all over the western third of the continent. The lure that drew them ever farther into the wilds was beaver, otter, and other fur-bearing animals, the pelts of which were highly prized in the capitals of Europe and other centers of wealth and fashion. As the sources of supply in the Rocky Mountain region were exhausted, the trappers pushed on toward the west and so eventually reached the shores of the Pacific.

The first "mountainman" to enter California was Jedediah Strong Smith. In 1826 the youthful Smith—he was then twenty-seven—led a party of trappers through the waterless plains of present-day Utah and Nevada. After a toilsome march across the Mojave Desert and over the San Bernardino Mountains the party reached the San Gabriel Mission in the southern part of the province. There they spent six weeks as guests of the hospitable padres while they recuperated from their ordeal. Then, having obtained new mounts and replenished their supplies, they crossed over the Tehachapi Range, thereby becoming the first overland party to enter the Central Valley from the United States.

The winter of 1826–27 was spent trapping in the valley, and in the early spring Smith and two companions set off for the fur-company rendezvous at Great Salt Lake, leaving the rest of the party behind. Instead of taking the southern route they had followed on the way west, the three, with nine horses and mules carrying food for men and animals, headed directly across the mountains. They safely gained the far side, but only after an exhausting eight-day struggle, much of it through deep snowdrifts. Theirs is believed to have been the first crossing of the Sierras.

But an even more difficult part of their journey lay ahead. For to reach the rendezvous hundreds of miles of arid countryside must be crossed. The little party entered that inhospitable land of barren hills and sandy, sage-covered plains with men and animals weakened from their passage over the mountains. As the days passed, food and water became a critical need. Because no wild game was encountered along the way, they were forced to kill their pack animals and subsist on their flesh. Much time was spent in fruitless searches for water. At one point in his later account of their ordeal Smith wrote:

At about 4 o'clock we were obliged to stop on the side of a sandhill under the shade of a small cedar. We dug holes in the sand and laid down in them for the purpose of cooling our heated bodies. After resting about an hour we resumed our wearisome journey, and traveled until 10 o'clock at night, when we laid down to take a little repose. . . . Our sleep was no respose, for tormented nature made us dream of things we had not, and for want of which it then seemed possible, or even probable, that we might perish in the desert. . . .

Twenty days after leaving the base of the Sierras, the half-starved trio reached the rendezvous at Great Salt Lake. Their arrival, in Smith's words, caused "a considerable bustle," for he and his companions "had been given up for lost."

After only a brief stay at the camp the indomitable leader again set out for California, taking with him eighteen trappers to reinforce the party left behind in the Central Valley. This journey too proved both difficult and hazardous. Instead of attempting another direct crossing of the mountains, he swung far to the south, and as he had done the previous year, entered California near its southern border.

All went well until the party reached the banks of the Colorado. Then, while they were crossing the river, a band of Navajo Indians launched a surprise attack. During the brief engagement ten of Smith's men were slain. The survivors who managed to gain the far side faced a desperate situation. All their horses and most of their provisions had been lost, and several hundred miles of mountains and desert separated them from the nearest California settlement. Traveling at night to avoid the extreme heat, the group reached the San Gabriel

Mission after an arduous march of nine and a half days.

There Father Sánchez, the priest who had befriended Smith on his first visit, again provided them with horses and food. After a brief rest, they crossed the Tehachapi Range into the Central Valley, where they joined the party Smith had left behind months earlier.

But their trials were far from over. When their leader, with three companions, visited the capital at Monterey seeking badly needed supplies, they were arrested as trespassers and thrown into jail. After several weeks of bargaining, Smith secured their release by promising to leave the province at the earliest opportunity. Having sold the furs the men in the valley had gathered during his absence, he used the proceeds to replace ammunition and other property lost during the Colorado crossing. He then rejoined the main party, and in December, 1826, prepared to return to Great Salt Lake.

Because the Sierra passes were blocked by snow, the expedition continued up the Sacramento Valley, bound for the Oregon country. During that part of the journey they encountered continuous rains. But the trapping was good, and they pushed on despite their discomfort. As they neared the northern end of the valley, however, they found that rain-swollen streams had flooded the entire countryside. Accordingly, they turned toward the coast and crossed the mountains of the Coast Range.

Breaking a trail through that heavily forested region—all the while beset by winter storms and in frequent danger from hostile Indians—was a tediously slow process. The party had progressed only as far as southwestern Oregon when disaster struck again. In early July of 1827 they were set on by a band

27

of Umpqua Indians, and all but Smith and two others were killed. The survivors made their way to the Hudson's Bay Company trading post at Fort Vancouver and reported the tragedy. A party was hastily organized and returned to the scene of the attack, where they buried the bodies of the victims and recovered traps, weapons, and other lost equipment, as well as the furs the men had gathered en route.

Jedediah Smith was undeterred by this latest catastrophe. Although he never returned to California, he continued to break new trails throughout the west for four years longer. Then, in the spring of 1831, he led a trading expedition into the Southwest, and while in advance of his party searching for water in the dry bed of the Cimarron, he was set on by a band of Comanches and slain. He was but thirty-two when his adventurous career ended.

The second fur-hunting party to lay traps in the Sacramento Valley was led by Ewing Young. Young and his party of about forty had set off from Taos, New Mexico, then an important trading center, in 1829. After trapping for some time in the region drained by the Salt River, the company had divided, one group returning to New Mexico while the others pushed on toward the west. This second section—which was headed by Young and included a twenty-year-old youth named Kit Carson—made their way into California, closely following the route Smith had taken two years earlier. During their stay, Young and his men ranged over much of central and northern California, gathering quantities of valuable furs.

These pioneer groups were soon followed by others, for

by then word had spread throughout the West that trapping was good along the Sacramento and its tributaries. As the sources of supply elsewhere became depleted, more and more of the fur traders followed the newly opened trails across the mountains. Among members of that wide-ranging company who trapped in California during the next few years were, to name but a few, William Wolfskill, Joseph Reddeford Walker, Zelas Leonard, James Clyman, and Jim Bridger.

In California the period of the fur hunters was brief. By the end of the 1830's the end was near, for the trappers had

done their work so well that the once numerous colonies of beaver and otter had been reduced to the point where the hunt for them was no longer profitable.

But as the fur trade was ending, a new sort of frontiersman had begun to appear in the Central Valley. Unlike the hunters and trappers, who spent only a few weeks or months there and then returned with their furs to trading posts beyond the mountains, the newcomers had a different end in view. They came as permanent residents, men who planned to settle on the fertile valley lands and "grow up with the country."

4

An Empire in the Wilderness

ONE morning in the summer of 1839 a group of about twenty left the sheltered waters of Yerba Buena cove at the tip of the San Francisco peninsula and headed up the bay. Once the three small craft—two open-deck schooners and a ship's pinnace—had rounded the western portal of the cove, those who had gathered for the departure trudged back over the sandy trail to the village, telling one another that the little party had embarked on a foolhardy venture and that it would come to no good.

The villagers had been saying much the same thing ever since Captain John Sutter had arrived in the bay a month earlier and announced that he planned to found a colony somewhere in the interior. They had pointed out that the region beyond the mountains was a primitive wilderness inhabited only by roving bands of Indians. A far more prudent course, they urged, would be for him to locate his settlement near the coast, where ample fertile land was to be had for the asking, and where his party would be not only safe from attack by

31

the natives but also close to the markets for the products he planned to raise.

The captain chose to ignore that advice. He had come to California with a definite purpose in mind, and he was determined to carry it out. His first move had been to visit Monterey and explain his bold plan to the governor, Juan Bautista Alvarado. The governor had listened with interest, and because he foresaw that such a settlement would help control the valley tribes, who had been making frequent raids on the herds of the *rancheros*, he gave the project his official sanction.

Elated by his success, Sutter had hurried back to Yerba Buena. There he chartered the three small ships from one of the local merchants, loaded his followers and such supplies as he had brought along on board, and on the morning of August 1, 1839, sailed into the unknown.

At the time he embarked on his California adventure, thirty-six-year-old John Augustus Sutter had already had a varied career. A former shopkeeper in the town of Burgdorf, Switzerland, the failure of his business there had forced him to flee to the United States to avoid being imprisoned for debt. On reaching this country he had gone directly to what was then the western frontier. There he spent a year in an unsuccessful farming venture in Missouri Territory, then joined a party of traders on two expeditions to Santa Fe. With the profits from these ventures he opened a trading post at the frontier town of Westport, on the site of present-day Kansas City.

It was during the second of his trips to the Southwest that the plan of someday establishing a colony in California first took shape in his mind. At Santa Fe he became acquainted with a former priest who had spent some time in that then remote Mexican possession. According to his friend, California was a land where the climate was mild the year around, the soil surpassingly productive, the natives friendly, and the rulers of the province both hospitable and generous. To the ambitious Sutter, this seemed to offer an opportunity to redeem himself for his failure as shopkeeper and farmer. Thereafter his one aim was to make his way to this favored land and there establish a community over which he could wield the power and authority his nature desired.

But in 1838 the journey from this Missouri frontier to California was one that few had the fortitude to undertake. For between the two points lay hundreds of miles of uninhabited prairies, lofty mountains, and all but impassable deserts. Up to that time only a few had passed that way, and all had encountered great hardship.

To reach his promised land, Sutter avoided the hazardous direct route and instead chose to follow a lengthy, roundabout course. In the spring of 1838 he joined a pack train sent out from Saint Joseph by the American Fur Company to carry supplies to the company's trappers in the Rocky Mountains. On reaching the rendezvous in late June he, taking an Indian youth as his sole companion, set off toward the northwest. After weeks of travel—first on foot, then in a canoe they themselves had built—the pair arrived at Fort Vancouver, the Hudson's Bay Company outpost on the Columbia River.

There Sutter had planned to board a ship for the voyage down the coast to California, but no ship headed in that direction was then in the port. After waiting several weeks, he took passage on a trading vessel bound for the Hawaiian Islands. At Honolulu he faced another long delay—time that he put to good use by recruiting men and supplies for his projected colony. After waiting several months for a California-bound ship, he and his party shipped out on the brig *Clementine*, which was setting off on a trading mission to the Russian settlements in Alaska. From there the *Clementine* sailed down the coast, and on July 1, 1839, dropped anchor in San Francisco Bay. Sutter's trip from the Missouri frontier had taken him more than a year.

A full month was spent making final preparations for the passage up the river, and on August 1 the little caravan pushed off. During the first stages of the voyage the party passed through familiar waters. Heading north and northeast, it crossed the upper arm of San Francisco Bay, rounded San Pablo point, and at the end of the second day, having bested the swift current of Carquinez Strait, entered the turbulent waters of Suisun Bay. There the ships put in at the Rancho el Pinole while their leader visited at the adobe ranch house of its owner, Ygnacio Martínez. The affable stranger speedily won the confidence of the rancher, who agreed to provide the new colony with horses, cattle, food, and other supplies once it had been established.

Soon after getting under way again, the expedition entered the maze of sloughs through which the Sacramento and San Joaquin rivers flow into the bay. Seated in the stern of the pinnace—which was rowed by four Kanakas he had brought from the Hawaiian Islands—Sutter led the way, exploring the winding waterways and tying bits of cloth to the branches

of trees in order to mark the way for those who followed.

After a long search, the channel of the Sacramento was located and the ascent of the meandering, tree-lined stream began. Once the low-lying delta was left behind, the river became a broad, placid stream, its banks a tangle of bushes and trailing vines above which rose tall poplars, valley oaks, and white-trunked cottonwoods.

For eight days the party pushed upstream. Each evening, while the others were on shore making camp, Sutter explored the surrounding countryside looking for a site for his colony. Few Indians were sighted on the lower river, but as the expedition neared the heart of the valley, they became more numerous.

One evening toward the end of the first week, while Sutter's men were making camp, they were startled to see a large group of natives emerge from the nearby woods. The Indians advanced rapidly, in full battle array. Those in the front rank,

35

whose bodies were daubed with brilliant red paint, were brandishing spears and gesticulating wildly.

Alarmed at their loud shouts and menacing behavior, the men seized their weapons and were preparing to defend themselves when their leader ordered them to withhold their fire. Himself unarmed, he advanced toward the oncoming group, shouting to make himself heard above the din. He addressed them as *amigos*, in the hope that some among them might understand the Spanish language.

That surmise proved correct. At a signal from their leader, the natives grew silent. Presently two braves stepped forward and identified themselves as former neophytes who had rejoined their tribe after the California missions had been closed a few years earlier. To them Sutter explained that his party had come on a peaceful errand, that they planned to make their home in the valley and wished to live on friendly terms with their Indian neighbors. Once this had been made clear to the others, the hostile demonstration ended. Sutter then presented their chief with a few small gifts, whereupon they withdrew.

The expedition pushed on upstream for several days longer, for Sutter was determined to explore the country thoroughly before choosing a site for his colony. But as the advance continued, members of the party grew restive. To the leader they pointed out that they were far beyond the last outposts of civilization and in constant danger of attack by the numerous bands of Indians sighted along the way. Finally, at the end of the eighth day—they had then reached a point near where the Feather River empties into the Sacramento—the discontented men confronted Sutter and demanded that he abandon his search.

Because some of his followers were close to mutiny, he reluctantly gave the order to turn about. All the next day they drifted downstream. When, toward evening, they neared the confluence of the Sacramento and American rivers, Sutter directed that they turn into the latter. A short distance beyond its mouth the boats put in at the south bank, and unloading operations began. Of the many possible sites Sutter had examined, this one had pleased him most.

Subsequent events were to prove that he had made a wise choice. The spot was in the heart of the valley, adjacent to two navigable rivers and surrounded by thousands of acres of fertile farmland, with here and there groves of huge oaks that would provide lumber for buildings and welcome shade during the hot summers.

Several Indian villages were in the vicinity of the landing place. The natives, attracted by the coming of the white men, gathered on the opposite bank in such numbers that as a precautionary measure Sutter had two small brass cannon he had brought with him set up in front of the camp.

The night passed without incident, but next morning an extraordinary event took place. As the *Isabella* and *Nicholas*, two of the ships that had brought the party upstream, swung into the river to begin the return trip, Sutter ordered the cannon fired as a parting salute.

The captain of the *Isabella* was an eighteen-year-old youth named William Heath Davis. Many years later Davis described what followed:

As the heavy report of the guns and the echoes died away, the camp of the little party was surrounded by hundreds of Indians, who were excited and astonished at the unusual sound. A large number of deer, elk, and other animals on the plains were startled, running to and fro, stopping to listen, full of curiosity and wonder, seemingly attracted and fascinated . . . while from the interior of the adjacent woods the howls of wolves and coyotes filled the air, and immense flocks of water fowl flew wildly about the camp.

Standing on the deck of the "Isabella," this remarkable sight made an indelible impression on my mind. This salute was the first echo of civilization in the primitive wilderness soon to become . . . a great agricultural and commercial center.

The party left behind when the launches sailed consisted of Sutter himself, three ex-sailors he had recruited at Honolulu, the Indian youth who had accompanied him from the Rocky Mountains, and twelve Hawaiians, two of whom were women. It was with the help of this oddly assorted company that Sutter hoped to carve out his inland empire.

In the beginning there seemed little likelihood that his ambitious plan could succeed. Aside from the small store of weapons, tools, and other supplies he had brought with him, he lacked nearly everything necessary to make the little community self-supporting. Among his pressing needs were food to sustain them until the first crops could be planted and harvested, horses and oxen to cultivate the newly laid-out fields, corn and wheat to plant in them, and a few head of cattle— the latter, he hoped, would form the nucleus of the great herds he visualized in the future. A further complication was that everything would have to be bought on credit, for Sutter was without funds to pay for his purchases.

These were obstacles that might well have daunted a less resolute man, but Sutter was undismayed. His first concern was to provide his party with temporary shelters until permanent quarters could be built. On an elevated spot a mile back from the river his Hawaiian workers put up several cabins of the type familiar in their homeland, having wooden frames and walls, and roofs of woven grass. Once these were finished, work began on a somewhat larger structure, which was built in the California manner, with thick walls made of sun-dried adobe bricks. It housed a workshop, a storeroom, a community kitchen, and Sutter's own quarters. It was completed and occupied by the time the winter rains began.

One means by which Sutter sought to raise the funds he desperately needed was by trapping beaver, the skins of which were in brisk demand and brought high prices. This venture was the first of many in which he enlisted the help of the valley Indians. With the cooperation of the chief of one of the neighborhood tribes, several groups of natives were organized and trained during the winter and dispatched on trapping expeditions up and down the valley. Meanwhile, other tribesmen were being taught to clear the land for the first crops, and still others began building a high adobe wall about the settlement to protect it from possible attack by hostile natives.

During his first year in the valley Sutter's difficulties mounted ever higher. His Indian trappers lacked both experience and proper equipment, and consequently, the number of furs they gathered fell far short of his expectations. Faced by that failure, he redoubled his efforts to find other sources of revenue, but here too progress was painfully slow. The merchants at Yerba Buena and Monterey and the cattle ranchers about the bay had little confidence in the success of his remote colony. Consequently, they responded cautiously, or not at all, to his repeated requests that they supply him—always on credit—with the materials he needed.

There was yet another complication. In California the ownership of land was limited to Mexican citizens, and to be eligible for citizenship a foreigner must have lived a full year in the province. Sutter was anxious to receive title to the land his colony occupied; so, as soon as twelve months had passed, he hurried to Monterey and applied for citizenship. His application was approved by the authorities, whereupon the former Swiss national became Don Juan Augusto Sutter, a full-fledged citizen of Mexico. Moreover, Governor Alvarado was so impressed by his new countryman that he appointed him his official representative in the Central Valley, with authority to enforce law and maintain peace and order.

Now that he was an official of his adopted country, Sutter's position was more secure. During the next several years New Helvetia—as he called his colony—grew rapidly in size and importance. Among those who joined his staff were a number of ex-sailors who had deserted their ships at Yerba Buena and Monterey and fled inland to avoid being forcibly returned. Some of these were trained artisans, and with their help Sutter was able to launch a variety of new industries. New Helvetia presently had a wood and metalworking shop, a tannery, a distillery, and a gristmill, with a number of others to follow.

However, it was the Indians who, then and later, made up most of his labor force. It was they who cleared the land, planted and harvested the crops, and tended the growing herds of livestock. The ultimate success of his enterprise was due in great measure to his ability to recruit large numbers of natives and teach them to perform such tasks. In his treatment of his Indian helpers he was by turns lenient and harsh. Those who did the work assigned them not only were given food and shelter but also were paid a daily wage. (Their "wages" were such, to them, highly prized objects as glass beads, pieces of bright-colored cloth, or similar trifles.) On the other hand, the punishment meted out for disobedience, thievery, or other wrongdoing was likely to be both prompt and severe.

In July, 1841, Sutter received title to the tract of land he had applied for a year earlier. In the California of his day land was considered to have little value, but even by the standards of that time, the grant was an extremely liberal one for it consisted of nearly fifty thousand acres. Three years later he was awarded a second grant, which more than doubled his holdings. He now owned two hundred square miles of farming and grazing land in the heart of the valley.

Another important event of 1841 was Sutter's purchase of Fort Ross, a settlement north of San Francisco Bay that the Russian-American Fur Company had founded in 1812. To buy this property—which the Russians were abandoning because their trappers had gathered all but a few of the once numerous sea otter in the area—he was obliged to assume a heavy debt. But in return, the purchase gave him many things, the lack of which had hampered the growth of his colony; among them were large herds of cattle, as well as badly needed lumber, tools, and agricultural implements. One particularly useful acquisition was a sturdy schooner, the *Constantine*. This Sutter put into service carrying passengers and freight to and from the settlements on the bay. The little vessel, which he renamed the *Sacramento*, was the first to make regular trips up and down the river.

Each year thereafter saw an increase in the size of the colony and the number of its activities. Sutter's Fort—it was called a fort because cannon were mounted on its high walls—occupied a space some 300 feet long and 160 feet wide. Ranged about the inner side of the wall were blacksmith and carpenter shops,

John Sutter

a textile mill, and rooms for a gunsmith, a shoemaker, and a cooper. A two-story adobe building, where Sutter lived and from which he directed his complex enterprise, stood in the center of the enclosure. Outside the wall were a gristmill, cattle corrals, and warehouses for storing wheat, corn, and other farm products. The tannery where cowhides (called "California banknotes" because they were then the chief medium of exchange in the province) were cured was a mile distant on the bank of the American River.

The 1840's were the most eventful decade in California history, and throughout those active years Sutter and his fort played an important role. During most of that period the fort was the only settlement in the entire Central Valley, and it was there that all but a few of the overland immigrants (who were arriving in ever-increasing numbers) made their way. All received a hearty welcome from the hospitable host. Those who planned to continue on to the coast were free to remain as long as they wished, and when they left they were provided with fresh horses to replace their spent animals. But many chose to remain at the fort, which was expanding so rapidly that Sutter had need of as many workers as he could find.

As his power and influence grew, Sutter took an increasingly active part in public affairs. In the fall of 1844 he recruited a nondescript "army" to help his friend Manuel Micheltorena, the current governor, put down a revolt in the southern end of the province. During a brief skirmish near the pueblo of Los Angeles Micheltorena's forces were defeated and Sutter himself was captured. After a few days in prison he was released and permitted to lead his dispirited followers back to

New Helvetia. That ended his military career. When, two years later, the long-threatened war between the United States and Mexico broke out, he put the resources of the fort at the disposal of the Americans, although he refused to take up arms against the Californians.

Following the conquest of the former Mexican province by the United States in 1846, a concerted migration to California got under way. All over the trans-Mississippi frontier, parties assembled in the spring of the following year and prepared to set off on the long overland trek. During the late summer and fall so many travel-weary immigrants straggled into the fort that facilities for caring for them were all but overwhelmed. But Sutter managed to provide food and shelter for all.

Many of the newcomers elected to remain in the valley. Some bought land Sutter offered them on generous terms and became farmers or cattle ranchers; others found employment in the mills and shops at the fort. There the influx of Yankee settlers ushered in a new period of growth and prosperity. For as the population of the valley grew, Sutter found a ready market for the products of his shops and fields and cattle ranges. To meet that need, and to prepare for greater demands in the future, he laid plans for further expansion.

One project he had had in mind for some time was the building of a sawmill to provide lumber for the settlers and for his own use. In the spring of 1847 he dispatched one of his helpers, a lanky Kentuckian named James Marshall, into the foothills to choose a site for the mill. By so doing, he, all unknowingly, set off a movement that was to draw to California the young and adventurous from all parts of the world.

5

Gold on the American River

THE spot Marshall selected for the future mill was in a picturesque valley on the south fork of the American River about forty-five miles northeast of the fort. Work began in the summer of 1847, and by mid-January of the following year the mill was nearly completed. All that remained was to deepen the ditch through which the water flowed back into the river after turning the wheel. To accomplish that, Marshall had left the intake gate open each night so the swiftly flowing water could wash the debris from the channel.

The story of the California gold discovery and its aftermath has been told many times: how, on the morning of January 24, Marshall chanced to notice a few flakes of yellow metal at the bottom of the tailrace; how, his curiosity aroused, he gathered up some of the shining particles, and placing them in the crown of his battered hat, carried them to the cabin where the millworkers were finishing their breakfast and announced: "Boys, I believe I've found a gold mine!"

The tall Kentuckian had indeed "found a gold mine." But

45

James Marshall

some time passed before the true importance of his discovery was recognized. For this was not the first time traces of gold had been found in California. Only six years earlier the major-domo at the San Gabriel Mission in the southern part of the province had happened on a ledge of gold-bearing quartz in a nearby canyon. That had stirred considerable interest among residents of the area, and a number of claims were staked out. But there, as was the case with other early-day gold mines, the yield was small, and after a few months the claims were abandoned.

Thus, when rumors of a new discovery, this time in the foothills of the Sierra, began to circulate, they aroused little interest. The Californians of the day were fully occupied with other and, to them, more important matters. The Treaty of

Guadalupe Hidalgo, by which the territory was ceded to the United States, had been signed on February 2, only nine days after Marshall's discovery. In recent months large parties of settlers had been arriving in California by both land and sea. With the population growing rapidly and all branches of trade active, few were tempted to leave the prospering towns and ranches to try their luck at so uncertain a venture.

This was particularly true of the fast-growing town on San Francisco Bay, the name of which had recently been changed from Yerba Buena to San Francisco. Despite evidence that gold in considerable quantity was being mined on the American River, San Franciscans remained skeptical. When, in its issue for March 15, 1848, the weekly *Californian* first announced the discovery, the news was relegated to a brief paragraph on the back page. Later that month Edward T. Kemble, editor of a rival journal, the *California Star*, which was San Francisco's first newspaper, paid a personal visit to the gold country. On his return he informed his readers that the report of the richness of the mines was, in his words, "a humbug."

Thus during the first several weeks it was only the workmen at the mill who profited by the discovery. At Sutter's urging, they had agreed to remain on the job until the mill was completed. However, a number of them became amateur miners during their off hours. Using whatever tools were at hand—in some instances they dug the metal from the exposed ledges with pocketknives—the amount of gold they gathered in a single day frequently exceeded their monthly wages.

News that strikes of such richness were being made could

not be long concealed. Once started, the word spread rapidly, first to Sutter's Fort and other points in the valley, then to all California. In San Francisco it was Sam Brannan, who had led a shipload of his fellow Mormons to California a few months earlier, who belatedly stirred the town to action. Returning from a trip to the mill, he rode down Montgomery Street holding aloft a bag of nuggets and shouting at the top of his ample lungs: "Gold! Gold on the American River!"

Brannan's announcement aroused intense excitement and set off a concerted rush to the gold country. Within a week the town was all but deserted. One writer thus described the scene:

By boat, by mule and horse, or on foot they went, all eager to reach the mines, fearing the gold would be gone before they could get there. . . . Business houses closed their doors. There was no service in the little church in the plaza and a padlock was on the door of the alcalde's [mayor's] office.

It was the same elsewhere in California. At the seaports, not only the townspeople joined the exodus; soldiers and sailors there deserted their posts, as did the crews of ships in the harbors. Only the old and feeble and the women and children remained behind.

The Californians who hastened to the gold fields in the spring and summer of 1848 were the advance guard of what was soon to become a worldwide movement. As the news spread abroad that fortunes in gold were being washed from the Sierra streams, it set in motion one of the greatest mass movements in history. First in the eastern part of the United States, then in foreign countries in both hemispheres, groups of adventurers banded together and prepared to set off for the new El Dorado.

Of the tens of thousands who reached California during the gold rush, the great majority came by water. By the summer of 1850 more than two hundred ships rode idly at anchor in San Francisco Bay, deserted alike by passengers and crews.

San Francisco, however, was not the end of their journey. For to reach the mines they must cross several hundred miles of uninhabited country, most of it without roads of any kind. Because the quickest and easiest means of travel to and from the interior had long been by water, all but a few of the argonauts chose to go by that route. Crowded into open-deck launches, ships' lifeboats, or whatever else was available, they crossed San Francisco, San Pablo, and Suisun bays, entered the Sacramento or San Joaquin river, and continued upstream to one or another of the landings that served as "jumping-off places" on the route to the mines. There they disembarked and, some afoot and others on muleback, crossed the floor of the valley to the eastern foothills.

Until the gold discovery, the only ship to ply the waters of the Sacramento on a regular schedule was Sutter's launch, the *Sacramento*, which made monthly round trips between San Francisco and the fort. But after the rush began, the once nearly deserted stream became a very lively place indeed. The diary of one argonaut, who made the ascent in the fall of 1848, records that during the daylight hours there were usually a dozen or more boats in sight, all heavily loaded with men and supplies. According to this writer, the river presented a picturesque scene after nightfall, with the lights from many campfires casting reflections on the water and illuminating the trunks of the cottonwoods. Others wrote of spending tedious hours marooned on sandbars waiting for the tide to turn, or searching for the channel of the uncharted, debris-strewn stream, and of sighting herds of deer and elk grazing in the distance, or immense flocks of ducks, geese, and other water-fowl. Few failed to mention the ravenous mosquitoes that swarmed about the camps in such numbers as to make sleep impossible.

Except for the newly founded town of Benicia on the north shore of Carquinez Strait, and the rancho of Ygnacio Martínez on the opposite side of the strait, the first miners to ascend the river encountered no settlements until they reached Sutter's Fort. The arrival there, first of scores, then of hundreds, of gold hunters speedily overran Sutter's small community.

Colonel R. B. Mason, the military governor of California, who visited the fort in the summer of 1848, found it a scene of feverish activity. Sutter's workers had all left for the mines; his mills and workshops were standing idle, and in the fields the unharvested crops were, in Mason's words, "being trampled by horses, cattle, and heedless men." His account continues: "Launches were discharging their cargoes at the Embarcadero. Carts were hauling goods to the fort, and several stores and a hotel already were established. Merchants paid Captain Sutter a monthly rental of $100 per room. While I was present a two-story house [Sutter's headquarters building] was rented at $500 a month as a hotel."

But Sutter's period of prosperity was brief. The fort was nearly two miles from the landing place, and with shiploads of men and material arriving there daily, most of his tenants moved to more convenient locations beside the river. By the end of 1848 two fast-growing towns had sprung up on the Sacramento: Sacramento City, on the site of the old landing site, and Sutterville, on higher ground a few miles downstream. Both prospered, and a spirited rivalry developed between them. But it was Sacramento City that became and remained the chief trading center for the northern mines. The future city was laid out in December, 1848, and the first lots were sold at auction the following January. A journalist who visited the spot less than nine months later wrote:

The growth and importance of this new settlement are among the marvelous things that are happening in this country. Last year I was at this place at the same season and there was not a house or even a tent there. . . . Now there is a town of 3,000 to 4,000 inhabitants, with a quay lined with fine buildings, streets laid out and with a large volume of business. . . . Thirty-five ships were at anchor, the smallest of which were fifty to sixty tons.

The rocketlike rise of Sacramento was typical of a number of other towns on the route to the gold fields. San Francisco, the port of entry for those who came by sea, was speedily transformed from a tiny frontier village to a sprawling city of many thousands. There was one period of several months when its population doubled every ten days. Such facilities as existed for housing and feeding the newcomers were quickly overwhelmed. Acres of tents spread over the outer sand hills, and the buildings about the plaza were taken over for offices, trading posts, bars, and gambling casinos.

51

Everything was in short supply, and prices reached fantastic heights. A vacant lot facing the plaza that a year earlier had been bought for $16.50 was sold in the spring of 1848 for $6,000, and before the end of the year resold for $45,000. A second lot, for which the original owner had paid $15.00, brought $45,000, and a third, which less than two years earlier had been traded for a barrel of whiskey, sold for $18,000.

Rentals followed the same upward spiral. A one-story building at a corner of the plaza was leased to a banker for $6,000 per month; one-room offices brought as much as $1,000 per month. The profits of the gambling casinos, which operated around the clock, were so high that their owners could afford to pay whatever was asked. One building rented for $180 *per day*, and space for a single faro table brought $30 for each twelve-hour shift.

Food prices were proportionately high. During a period of scarcity in the fall of 1848 eggs sold for one dollar each and potatoes and onions for $1.50 per pound. One early-day restaurant boasted the luxury of a printed bill of fare. It listed these items: "Bean soup, $1; hash, low grade, 75c; hash, 18-carat, $1; beef, plain, $1; beef, with one potato, $1.50; baked beans, plain, 75c; baked beans, greased, $1; two potatoes, 50c; two potatoes, peeled, 75c; rice pudding, 75c."

But with fortunes in gold being washed from the Sierra streams, costs were a lightly regarded detail. By the end of 1848 parties of prospectors, fanning out from the site of the original discovery, had begun to reveal the true extent of the gold fields. Hardly a week passed but that word of new strikes, some of them surpassingly rich, drifted down to the valley, setting off new rushes to those areas. So rapidly was the gold country explored and populated that by midsummer of 1849 thousands of claims were being worked from Mariposa on the south to the Shasta and Trinity river districts, a distance of some 250 miles.

To serve the widely separated mining camps, a number of new towns sprang up on the banks of the Sacramento and the San Joaquin. Sacramento City remained the chief trading center for the entire upper end of the valley. However, as new mining districts were opened farther north, ships began operating on the upper Sacramento and its tributaries, thereby shortening the distance men and supplies had to be transported by land. One of the first of the new river towns was Marysville, which owed its rapid rise to the fact that it was the

head of navigation on the Feather River and adjacent to a group of prosperous gold camps. The town was laid out in 1850; two years later its streets were lined with substantial brick buildings, its docks crowded with shipping. Each morning a long line of stages assembled in front of the town's principal hotel, preparing to leave for one or another of such picturesquely named gold camps as—to name but a few—Bidwell's Bar, French Corral, Rabbit Creek, Oregon Hill, Poker Flat, and Rough and Ready.

In March, 1848, less than two months after the discovery at Sutter's Mill, the finding of rich placers near the base of Mount Shasta set off a rush to the far northern end of the Sacramento Valley. Soon claims were being worked in the many streams, gulches, and canyons of the rugged back country. This in turn led to a heavy traffic on the upper river, with a fleet of sternwheel steams pushing ever farther upstream, carrying men and supplies toward Shasta City, Scott's Bar, Weaverville, and other towns in the Shasta-Trinity area. First Colusa, then Benton City, then Tehama, and finally Red Bluff —the last-named 150 miles above Sacramento—became the head of navigation. Each enjoyed a brief period of activity, then declined as the channel beyond was cleared of sandbars, snags, and other obstructions, permitting the ships to advance a few miles farther.

Red Bluff remained for many years the northern terminus of traffic on the river. By the summer of 1852 the town had three large stores, two hotels, two boardinghouses, a physician (who was also the town druggist), a number of cattle corrals, and a barbershop. In January of the following year, a correspondent for a San Francisco newspaper reported that on a walk from the landing to the business center he counted "140 pack mules and 15 teams, loaded, and making their way to the interior."

In the beginning, the towns on the Sacramento and its tributaries were little more than way stations on the route to the mines, points where men and supplies left the river and continued on by land. As time passed, however, the richer placers were "worked out," and all but a few of the miners abandoned their claims. Some returned to their former homes; others joined new gold rushes to British Columbia, Australia, and other distant points; and still others, attracted by the abundance of fertile land in the valley, settled there and became farmers.

The great cattle ranches were gradually broken up and put to other uses. Wheat, corn, and other field crops were planted, orchards and vineyards set out, dairies and truck farms established. Before many years had passed the former river landings had become the commercial and social centers of flourishing farming communities, complete with churches, schools, libraries, theaters, and all the other features of long-established American towns.

6

Paddle-Wheel Days

ALTHOUGH sailing ships were a familiar sight on the river in gold-rush days and later, it was a fleet of sturdy, wood-burning steamers that carried most of the heavy traffic.

The forerunner of the fast and elegant "floating palaces" that were to ply California's inland waterways for nearly a century was the Russian-built schooner *Sitka*, which made the trip from San Francisco to Sutter's Fort late in 1847. Her ascent of the Sacramento was the *Sitka's* most ambitious cruise. She left Yerba Buena cove on the morning of November 29 and arrived at Sutter's embarcadero on the afternoon of December 5, the 125-mile voyage having taken a few hours less than a week. Her return trip must have been made at an even more leisurely pace, for it is said that an oxcart that left the embarcadero at the same time reached Benicia four days ahead of the primitive little steamer.

The *Sitka* did not attempt a second ascent of the Sacramento, and nearly two years passed before the sound of churning paddle wheels again broke the solitude of the river. Then, early in 1849, two other steamers made their inaugural runs. The first was the *Lady Washington*, a light-draft stern-wheeler that had been built on the East Coast, shipped around the Horn in the hold of a sailing ship, and reassembled at Sacramento City. During August two others, appropriately named the *Pioneer* and the *Sacramento*, were put on the river run. Like the *Lady Washington*, they were small craft of limited capacity and uncertain performance; both had been brought out in parts from the Atlantic seaboard.

Meanwhile, at Washington, D.C., steps were being taken to provide better and faster means of communication with the country's new West Coast possession. In March, 1847, Congress passed an act authorizing the formation of two steamship lines, one on the Atlantic and the other on the Pacific, with a crossing at Panama, and granting their operators a liberal subsidy for carrying the mails. On the Pacific side the contract was awarded the Pacific Mail Steamship Company, which agreed to provide two sailings per month between Panama and San Francisco, with intermediate stops at Acapulco and San Diego.

To inaugurate service on the Pacific, three steamers were built, the *California*, *Oregon*, and *Panama*. First to be commissioned was the *California*, a 1,050-ton side-wheeler with accommodations for sixty first-class passengers and a hundred and fifty in the forward cabin and steerage. She sailed from New York in early October, 1848, with only seven passengers on board, and after rounding South America, dropped anchor off Panama City in mid-January, 1849.

There a surprise awaited her, for lining the beach was a

57

crowd of close to a thousand men, all clamoring to come on board. The reason for their presence was soon explained. During the *California*'s months-long cruise, the gold rush had got under way on the East Coast. Already shiploads of miners were disembarking at Chagres and hurrying across the isthmus in the hope of finding a ship that would speed them to California.

Taking on board 365 passengers—which was nearly twice her normal capacity—the *California* continued up the coast. The final leg of the long voyage was beset by misfortune. Many passengers fell ill, some from fever contracted on the isthmus, others because of the overcrowded conditions on board. A shortage of food and water added to the distress. Then, while off the California coast, the coal ran out and the fittings of cabins had to be torn out and burned to keep steam up in the boilers. This enabled the ship to reach Monterey, where a supply of wood was taken on, and eventually, on the last day of February, she passed through the Golden Gate. No sooner had she anchored off Yerba Buena cove than the crew joined the passengers in a headlong rush to the mines.

Meanwhile, word had reached the East Coast that an acute shortage of transportation facilities existed on the Sacramento and San Joaquin rivers. Shipowners made haste to take steamers off their regular runs, and after strengthening and provisioning them for the around-the-Horn voyage, dispatched them for California. Unlike the *California*, which left New York with cabins nearly empty, those that followed were loaded to their fullest capacity. So great was the demand that passenger fares and freight rates soared to such heights that in some instances the profits from a single round trip are said to have equaled the cost of the vessels.

On reaching California, some steamers were put on the San Francisco–Panama run, while others entered the coastwise trade, serving towns in California and Oregon. The majority, however, joined the heavy traffic flowing to and from Sacramento, Stockton, and other interior points. One of the latter was a Boston-built side-wheeler, the 750-ton *Senator*, which arrived in the fall of 1849 and quickly became a favorite with travelers to and from the gold towns. For close to two decades she was a familiar sight on the bay and river. During all that period she maintained a fast schedule, leaving her San Francisco wharf at two P.M. every second day, making the 125-mile passage to Sacramento in under ten hours, and casting off on her return trip at nine the next morning.

But speed was not the only advantage the *Senator* enjoyed over her rivals. Passengers were attracted, too, by her handsomely appointed cabins and her spacious dining salon and other public rooms. Such luxurious accommodations made a strong appeal to the affluent miners, who at times paid as much as forty dollars for a berth in one of her elegant staterooms. So popular was she with the traveling public that during her first years on the river she is said to have earned a profit of sixty thousand dollars a month.

But the *Senator* and her early-day competitors did not long enjoy a monopoly on the lucrative river trade. By the end of 1850 a fleet of nearly fifty steamers was churning the inland waterways. The larger ships shuttled between San Francisco and Sacramento or Stockton, with an intermediate stop at

59

Benicia on the upper bay. Meanwhile, a group of small, flat-bottom stern-wheelers, many of them drawing less than two feet of water when fully loaded, were put in service on the upper Sacramento and its larger tributaries. Battling sandbars and other obstructions in the shallow channel, they pushed ever farther upstream with men and supplies bound for the northern mines.

As the number of steamers on the river grew, the competition brought about a gradual reduction in passenger fares and freight rates. Whereas during 1849 and much of 1850 passage between San Francisco and Sacramento had cost an average of twenty-five dollars per person—plus ten dollars if one occupied a stateroom—by the end of 1850 fares had fallen to less than half that amount. Indeed, there was one period in the fall of that year when the rival steamers were offering passage from San Francisco to Sacramento at the bargain rate of one dollar.

Such ruinous rate wars ended in 1854, when a number of owners joined together and organized the California Steam Navigation Company, which was to control a major share of shipping on the river for nearly two decades.

The flagship of the company's fleet was the *Chrysopolis*, a graceful 235-foot side-wheeler that went into service in 1860. Her powerful engines and narrow hull made her the fleetest craft on the river; she once made the passage from Sacramento to San Francisco in five hours and nineteen minutes, a record that was to stand for many years. Because of her superior speed, the "Slim Princess," as she was called, replaced the older *Senator* as the favorite of the traveling public. During the

fifteen years she remained on the Sacramento run she maintained so punctual a schedule that residents along the way were said to regulate their watches by her passage up and down the river.

Because the faster steamers attracted the most patronage, there was strong urge to operate them at unsafe speeds and so complete their runs ahead of their competitors. One result of this emphasis on speed was a long series of disasters. Collisions were frequent, most of them caused by crowded conditions on the narrow, unmarked channel. By far the most serious wrecks, however, were caused by the explosion of the laboring ships' overburdened boilers. When that happened there was usually a heavy loss of life among passengers and crews. During the first several years such accidents were so frequent that laws were passed imposing strict controls on shipowners by state and federal agencies. Once they went into effect, safety returned to the river.

When the transcontinental railroad was completed in 1869, Sacramento became its western terminus and remained so for several years. There passengers bound for San Francisco left the overland trains and crossed the levee to waiting steamers. The accounts of early-day travelers rarely fail to express surprise at finding ships of such size and luxury at what to them was still a remote frontier town. An English writer, W. F. Rae, who arrived in 1870, described the steamer he boarded at Sacramento as "large, commodious, and luxurious."

The upper saloon [he continued] resembles a large hall in an English country home, furnished in the style and with the taste of a splendid drawing-room. . . . The dining saloon is in the lower part of the vessel. This is a lofty, airy, and well-lit apartment. During the day the light streams in through large windows; after nightfall many gas jets make it as brilliant as if the sun shone. . . . On the deck there is ample space for the comfortable accommodation of those who delight in walking or sitting in the open air. The return journey is made at night, and then the comforts of a well-appointed state-room may be had for a small extra payment.

The passenger steamers on the San Francisco–Sacramento run were the aristocrats of the river trade, but they bore only a minor share of the traffic on the Sacramento. As they made their way up and down the river, their paddle wheels turning rapidly to maintain their fast schedules, they left numerous lesser craft bobbing in their wake. Many of the latter were stern-wheelers whose flat bottoms permitted them to operate in waters that were far too shallow for the larger steamers.

On their passage up from San Francisco, these small carriers made frequent stops to land passengers and merchandise at one or another of numerous landings along the river. On their return trips they picked up miscellaneous cargoes of hay, fruit, vegetables, or other farm products consigned to produce merchants in San Francisco. Because of their light draft and maneuverability, they were able to land virtually anywhere on the river itself or in the narrow sloughs that flow into it.

By the mid-1850's many of the richer placer mines had been stripped of their treasure, and this had brought about a gradual falling off in the amount of traffic on the river. But not for long. For the decline of mining in the foothills was accompanied by the rise of agriculture in the valley, and as the farms and orchards and cattle ranches grew in number, so did the amount of shipping needed to convey their products.

In the middle 1860's the flow of traffic on both the Sacramento and the San Joaquin increased even further. The soil and climate of California's Central Valley were found to be ideal for the growing of a variety of wheat that could be shipped without damage on long sea voyages. Once that became known, so much land was planted to the profitable crop that California was soon producing a major part of the world's supply of wheat. Between 1865 and 1890 the yearly harvest rose from less than six million bushels to more than fifty million.

Each fall immense quantities of sacked wheat were loaded from the fields where the wheat was grown onto the decks of barges or steamers and brought down to deep water on the Carquinez Strait, which connects San Pablo and Suisun bays. There it was graded and stored, then transferred to fast sailing ships that carried it to all parts of the world. So large did this operation become that during the heyday of the wheat trade a continuous line of docks and warehouses occupied both sides of the strait for a distance of several miles.

The wheat-growing era lasted well into the 1890's. Then, as the century drew to a close, production fell off rapidly, the chief reason being that the custom of planting the fields to the same crop year after year had exhausted the soil. This, together with the development of new wheat-growing centers in the Argentine, Australia, and elsewhere, brought the California operation to an end. Thereupon the great wheat farms, like the cattle ranches before them, one by one were subdivided and put to other uses.

Although the once numerous barges, their decks piled high with sacked wheat, were seen no more, traffic on the river remained heavy for some years longer. Fast, well-appointed steamers provided daily service between San Francisco, Sacramento, and Stockton, and a fleet of small stern-wheelers, combination passenger-and-freight carriers, made regular trips on the upper Sacramento and its tributaries.

To many who lived close to the river the visits of these versatile little ships were a decided convenience. Without them it would have been necessary for the farmers to haul their produce to the nearest towns—and the roads were usually few and bad, and the towns far apart. Moreover, during the early period, when floods were frequent, there were occasions when the entire countryside was under water for weeks at a time.

When that happened, scores of families, and sometimes entire villages, were forced to depend on the ubiquitous riverboats for food for themselves and their livestock.

Another sort of vessel that was welcomed wherever it went, and particularly at more remote sections of the river, was the so-called store ship. These small steamers, which have been described as "floating variety stores," made regular trips up and down the Sacramento, stopping at isolated farming communities and bartering manufactured goods for home-grown products. The store ship announced its approach by three long blasts of its whistle, whereupon those who lived in the vicinity hurried down to the landing place and stocked up on groceries, clothing, and whatever else was needed, paying for their purchases with boxes of fruit, dairy products, sacks of

potatoes, and the like—sometimes even with a pig, a calf, or a crate of live chickens.

Sometime in the early 1890's yet another picturesque feature was added to life on the river, when the manager of a theatrical company chartered one of the light-draft stern-wheelers, and by converting the cargo space on the lower deck into a theater, made her the Far West's first—and only—showboat. Little is known today of this unique little vessel, and it could not have operated for more than a season or two. But there is a record of its having made a number of trips on both the Sacramento and Feather rivers, bringing welcome entertainment to the many small communities along the way. At the towns, the company took over a lodge room or other hall and remained several days; where there were no such facilities, one-night stands were made aboard the ship itself. The performances were of the type known as "medicine shows"; that is, during breaks in the performances, hucksters passed up and down the aisles peddling bottles of various cure-alls.

The completion of the transcontinental railroad in 1869 and its extension to San Francisco and Oregon in the early and middle 1870's brought about marked changes in the nature of traffic on the Sacramento. But although the river lost much of its trade to its new and faster rival, many products of the valley continued to be shipped by water. Thus the commerce on the river has grown steadily from year to year, and today is the largest in its history.

7

Taming the River

RAINFALL is abundant in some parts of California and extremely light in others. The far northern counties average from seventy to eighty inches annually—compared to less than twenty inches in the state as a whole—and the higher peaks of the Sierra and Cascade ranges often receive as much as four hundred inches of snow in a single season. Moreover, this heavy precipitation is confined almost entirely to the period from November to April; during the remainder of the year rain rarely falls.

One result of these conditions is that, until comparatively recent times, the level of water in the Sacramento was likely to be either dangerously high or inconveniently low, depending on the season. During the winter months it frequently overflowed its banks and flooded the surrounding countryside. Then, during the long, dry summers, its level sometimes declined to the point where it was closed to navigation over much of its length.

The first attempts to regulate the flow of the Sacramento, and so prevent the recurring periods of abnormally high or low water, were made as early as 1849. But it proved to be a long and complicated task, and more than half a century passed before the river was made both safe and navigable the year around.

Meanwhile, prolonged winter storms, or the runoff of melting snow in the mountains, regularly transformed the usually tranquil stream into a raging torrent, bringing on a series of disastrous floods. The river was particularly vulnerable to damage from that source, for over much of its course the land was only a few feet above its surface. At such points even a moderate rise in the water level caused it to spread over wide areas, washing out crops, drowning livestock, and engulfing towns and villages in its path.

Sacramento, the largest settlement in the valley, was a frequent victim of the river's periodic rampages. The first of many floods that were to plague the city during the next several decades took place in January, 1849. One writer who witnessed the catastrophe thus described the scene: "The country presented a sheet of water for miles around, save here and there a knoll or ridge, and the dotting of trees and houses. Hundreds of animals were drowned; some lives were lost, and an enormous amount of property was destroyed." A year later, weeks of heavy rain in the upper valley brought on a second major flood. Again the waters covered the entire city, rising to the second story of buildings in the business district and forcing the populace to flee to higher ground at Sutter's Fort and elsewhere.

Hardly had the citizens repaired the damage from this January, 1850, flood when a new series of storms again raised the river to threatening heights. Faced by this emergency, the residents, under the leadership of Hardin Bigelow, a local merchant who had lived in the Mississippi delta, hastened to the riverbank and prepared for battle. By working through several days and nights throwing up a temporary levee, they managed to fend off the cresting water and avert a new disaster. Because of Bigelow's part in that endeavor, the grateful citizens made him the first mayor of the newly chartered city.

At the same election the voters approved a bond issue of $250,000 to strengthen the levee and increase its height. Work on that ambitious project, which involved the moving of 120,000 cubic yards of earth, began in September, 1850. When completed, it was nine miles long and from three to twenty feet high, and served to protect the city during the mild winter of 1851–52. In the spring of 1853, however, the pressure of the water caused a section of the levee on the American River side to collapse, sending huge masses of water cascading down into the city. For several weeks thereafter the streets were impassable by any means except rowboats. This latest disaster led to a further extension and strengthening of the city's levee system—a work that was carried on almost continuously for nearly a decade. Thereafter, the city was comparatively safe, for although it was several times placed in jeopardy during subsequent periods of high water—notably in the spring of 1862—the threat of major floods gradually subsided.

Sacramento's long struggle to ward off the swollen river was duplicated at a number of other places in the valley. Levees were built at Marysville, Yuba City, Colusa, and other towns on the upper Sacramento and its tributaries, all of which had experienced damaging floods. The same was true of many farming communities. There the settlers sought to protect their homes and fields and livestock by putting up their own dikes, only to have them washed out during the next season of high water. Once the inadequacy of such individual efforts had been demonstrated, the farmers pooled their labor, and levee-building became a community enterprise.

But it presently became clear that to confine the river to its normal channel over its entire length would require the building and maintenance of several hundred miles of levees. This was a task far too large and complex to be carried out by the methods formerly used. Thereupon flood control on the Sacramento became the responsibility of state and federal agencies. The first bill appropriating funds for that purpose was passed by the California legislature in 1854, and was followed by others. Later the U.S. Corps of Army Engineers took over, and an extensive program of levee-building got under way. It has continued ever since, and as the work progressed the threat of damaging floods declined each year and finally disappeared entirely. Today it is possible to ride for many miles on roads atop the river's magnificent system of levees, and from that vantage point to look down at the peacefully flowing river on one side and, on the other, at hundreds of acres of prosperous farms and orchards.

Another work that added substantially to the agricultural wealth of the valley was the reclamation of nearly half a million acres of potentially rich land in the Sacramento–San Joaquin delta. The region is one of low-lying islands, criss-

A river levee

crossed by shallow sloughs, the soil of which, when cleared and drained and protected by dikes, yields prodigious crops. To encourage settlers to take up land there and make it productive, the state advertised the semi-submerged islands for sale at bargain prices—in some instances for as little as one dollar per acre. Those who accepted the offer faced a long and arduous task. For before the first crops could be planted, the land had to be cleared of a dense growth of tules and protected by dikes and drainage canals. Then, as often as not, their many months of hard labor were swept away in a few hours, when winter floods washed out the dikes, burying the fields under several feet of water and ruining the crops.

However, those who persevered were richly rewarded. Once higher and stronger dikes had made the land secure, virtually everything planted in the fertile peat soil bore profusely. Today the once useless delta land is the most valuable in the entire Central Valley, its large, intensively cultivated farms producing a major share of the state's supply of asparagus, beans, onions, celery, potatoes, and other vegetables.

While the long and ultimately successful battle to confine the river to its normal channel was being waged, another important work was under way: that of clearing the stream of numerous hazards to shipping and making it both safe and navigable at all seasons of the year. This, too, was a long-drawn-out process. When the gold rush began there were, of course, no charts or lights or buoys to mark the way for the hundreds of ships carrying men and supplies to the mines.

The consequence was that for many months all was confusion. The accounts of travelers tell of days spent in the meandering sloughs of the delta, searching for the mouth of the Sacramento, and of seemingly interminable delays caused by straying from the channel and running around in shallow water. Sandbars and submerged tree trunks were another ever-present hazard, as was the danger of having the steamers' paddle wheels fouled by masses of debris floating downstream during periods of high water.

The rainless months of summer and fall posed problems of a different sort. At such seasons the water was frequently so low that, over much of its length, the river was closed to all but the smallest steamers. Many of the latter drew so little water that, according to tradition, they were able to operate "wherever the ground was a little damp."

That the versatile little ships were able to make regular trips on the upper Sacramento and Feather rivers even when the water was abnormally low is a tribute to their sturdy construction as well as to the resourcefulness of their officers and crews. On their passage upstream they were so heavily loaded that they sometimes ran aground at shallow spots in the channel. When that happened, the usual procedure was to attach a line to the trunk of a tree some distance ahead and to wind the other end about the ship's capstan. The pull on the line, together with the force of the churning paddle wheel, was usually enough to draw the steamer over the obstruction. But there were times when even such measures failed, and service on the upper river had to wait for the winter rains.

Efforts to speed the flow of traffic on both rivers commenced soon after the gold rush began. Initially this was limited to marking the channel and clearing it of submerged logs, and was done by the shipowners themselves. Later the Army Engineers took over, and under their direction detailed charts were prepared, buoys and other aids to navigation installed, and shallow spots in the channel deepened by means of dredgers. Later still, existing sloughs were dredged out and new channels dug that eliminated curves in the meandering rivers. By that means the distance between San Francisco, Sacramento, and Stockton was shortened by many miles. The result of such work, which has continued ever since, is that today the two inland cities of Sacramento and Stockton are regular ports of call for the merchant ships of many nations.

By 1855 most of the free gold had been washed from the Sierra streambeds, and as placer mining declined, two other methods of extracting the metal came into use. One was quartz mining, which involved the building of stamp mills where gold embedded in rock was recovered by feeding the ore into crushers, or "stamps." Quartz mining continued throughout the gold country for many years, and is still being carried on at a number of points.

The second method, known as hydraulic mining, also began in the mid-1850's. By that means, streams of water under high pressure were played on the gold-bearing deposits, washing whole hillsides down into sluices, where the metal was recovered. At first such operations were on a small scale and aroused no concern in the valley. But once it had been demonstrated that low-grade ore which could not be successfully worked by other means yielded handsome profits by this method, its use spread rapidly. By 1860 more than a score of hydraulic mines was operating from Mariposa north to

Downieville. Each year thereafter hundreds of acres of once pleasant countryside were reduced to rubble under the assault of the powerful jets of water.

Meanwhile, the streams flowing into the Sacramento Valley had become clogged with mud and debris from the hydraulic mines, causing many of them to overflow their banks and bury nearby fields and orchards under several feet of clay and gravel. But the damage done was not confined to the destruction of farmlands in the valley, serious as that was. Vast amounts of sand and silt were carried into the Sacramento itself, muddying its waters and decreasing the depth of the channel. This gradual filling of the river—between 1855 and 1870 its normal level rose more than five feet—not only seriously interfered with navigation but also made it necessary to build higher dikes and levees to protect against winter floods.

Once the people of the valley realized the seriousness of this threat, they banded together, organized the Anti-Debris Association, and began a long campaign to protect their property from further damage. From 1860 on, bills to prohibit hydraulic mining, or failing that, to prevent the dumping of waste material into the mountain streams, were regularly introduced into the legislature. The bills were vigorously opposed by the mining interests, and for some time were uniformly defeated. But in the late 1870's laws were finally passed which restricted hydraulic mining to certain localities and forbade the pollution of the waterways. Although hydraulic mining continued on a limited scale for some years thereafter, it no longer posed a serious threat to landowners in the valley. Their long battle had been won.

8

Water for the Thirsty Land

THE gold discovery had, of course, a profound effect on all phases of life in California, but nowhere did it bring about greater or more lasting changes than in the Central Valley.

Because of it, the region's transition from a remote and sparsely settled frontier land to a well-ordered and flourishing farming community—a process that in the ordinary course of events would have taken two or three decades—was accomplished in as many years.

It was the presence of thousands of gold hunters in the foothills to the east and north that accounted for the rapid rise of agriculture in the valley. The miners produced little in the way of food, for either themselves or their animals, and as the population of the gold towns grew, it created a ready market, at increasingly high prices, for farm products of every kind. So great was the demand, and so attractive the chances of profit, that many newcomers gave up their plan of seeking fortunes in the mines and became farmers instead. Soon they were joined by others who had failed to locate claims.

During the first several years only lands bordering on the rivers were put under cultivation, for there the water was close to the surface, and virtually anything planted yielded abundant crops. But the amount of such land was limited. Once it had all been occupied, attention turned to the many thousands of acres elsewhere in the valley that lacked only water to make them equally productive. Thereupon a movement got under way that in the years to come was to add immeasurably to the agricultural wealth of the region. This was accomplished by tapping the river and foothill streams and, by means of dams and ditches, bringing life-giving water to the districts that formerly had served only as winter grazing ranges for cattle.

To be sure, the farmers of the Central Valley were not the first Californians to increase the productivity of their land by that means; irrigation had been practiced in the fields and gardens of the Spanish missions nearly a century earlier. But that had been a small-scale operation, whereas here its use spread until it eventually covered hundreds of square miles.

To bring that about, the usual procedure was for small groups of farmers living in the same neighborhood to form irrigation districts and by their joint labor dig the ditches needed to bring water from a nearby river. Later, the privately owned properties were taken over by larger companies. These companies built dams, storage reservoirs, and a network of canals that distributed water over large areas. For that service the farmers paid a fee for each acre-foot of water used—an acre-foot being the amount needed to cover an acre of ground to a depth of one foot.

With the rapid spread of irrigation, and a dependable supply of water, hundreds of acres of semi-arid land were put under cultivation. The former cattle ranches were subdivided into smaller units, some planted to hay, grain, and other field crops. Others became truck farms supplying vegetables for the booming markets, and on still other lands orchards and vineyards were set out.

But while the boon of irrigation enormously increased the productivity of the land, as time passed the use of water for that purpose created a number of perplexing problems, some of which were not resolved for many years. Much of the controversy that arose had to do with what is called riparian

rights; that is, the right of landowners to take water from streams that pass through, or are adjacent to, their property. For example, under riparian rules, owners are forbidden to draw off so much water as to leave an insufficient supply—or none at all—for their neighbors farther downstream.

During the first few years there was ample water for all who had need of it. As the number and size of the irrigation districts grew, however, so did the amount of water withdrawn from the stream. The result was that in some areas serious shortages developed during the planting and growing seasons. Thereupon a campaign was commenced at Sacramento to have legislation passed designed to conserve water during the dry summer months and to assure its equitable distribution.

There were other complications. So much water was soon being diverted from the Sacramento and the streams that flow into it that the level of the water frequently declined to the point where it seriously interfered with shipping. Moreover, at times when the river was abnormally low, saltwater from the bay was drawn upstream, threatening the fertile farmlands of the delta.

Because it was recognized that the prosperity of the valley depended to a great extent on the availability of water, plans to prevent its waste and to put it to the most productive uses were started quite early. In 1854 the legislature passed an act creating the Board of Water Commissioners to study the problem and suggest possible solutions. On the board's recommendation, a bill was passed providing that users of water for irrigation, mining, and other purposes be required to return the surplus to the streams from which it was originally taken. Thereafter hardly a year passed but that bills were introduced into the legislature dealing with one phase or another of this troublesome subject, whether it be levee-building, dredging or other flood-control devices, or irrigation, hydraulic mining, or shipping.

Although a wide variety of such measures was initiated and carried out during the first half-century after California became a state, all but a few dealt with matters pertaining only to the northern half of the Central Valley; that is, to the river itself, its tributaries, and the lands bordering on them. But soon after the twentieth century began, a bold new water plan was proposed—one that, if it could be carried out, would confer lasting benefits not only on the Central Valley but also on the lands that lie south of the Tehachapis.

The Central Valley Project, as it came to be called, has been described as "the most extensive water transport system in the history of the world." Its chief purpose is to store northern California water—this part of the state each winter receives far more than can be used—and by means of a complex system of aqueducts, tunnels, and pumping stations to deliver the surplus to parts of the state where rain rarely falls.

A work of that size required careful planning, for each phase of the operation had to be on a vast scale. More than a decade passed before the plan was found to be feasible from both the engineering and financial standpoints. Once that had been determined, the Central Valley Project Act was passed by Congress in 1937 and necessary funds appropriated for it. Actual construction began the following year and still continues.

The first major unit of the system was Shasta Dam, which lies beyond the northern end of the valley, near the headwaters of the Sacramento. Its building began in 1938, and it was completed seven years later. Some indication of its size and height may be gained from the fact that water flowing over its spillway falls a distance more than three times that of Niagara Falls, and enough concrete was used in its construction to build a three-foot-wide sidewalk around the world at the equator. The 602-foot-high barrier forms an artificial lake 35 miles long, with 365 miles of shoreline. Finally, as the water is released from the lake, it is fed through penstocks at a powerhouse at the base of the dam, where enough hydroelectric power is generated to meet the needs of a city of half a million.

Large as it is in all its dimensions, Shasta Dam has been dwarfed by a second dam, this one built across a canyon of the Feather River near the town of Oroville, some ninety miles to the southeast. The Oroville Dam is 770 feet high, a mile and a half long, and contains eighty million cubic yards of earth and rock, making it by far the largest earth-fill dam ever built. It forms a many-armed lake that, when filled to capacity, holds 3.5 million acre-feet of water. The hydroelectric plant at the base of the dam is on a comparable scale.

Meanwhile, as dams and powerhouses were being built on all the larger streams flowing down from the mountains, work was progressing on the second phase of the project: that of distributing the stored water to those parts of the Central Valley that needed only the benefits of irrigation to transform them into productive farming communities. This, too, is an

immensely large and complex undertaking, one that includes
hundreds of miles of aqueducts, pipelines, and tunnels, as well
as a number of great pumping plants.

One of the keystones of the distribution system is the Cross
Delta Channel, which diverts water from the Sacramento River
and carries it across the Sacramento–San Joaquin delta, where
part is emptied into the Contra Costa Canal. This provides
water for municipal, industrial, and irrigation purposes in the
populous region that lies to the west and south. The remainder
flows into the pumping station at Tracy. There six centrifugal
pumps, each with a capacity of a third of a million gallons
per minute, lift the water 196 feet above sea level and empty
it into the Delta-Mendota Canal, which carries it down the
western side of the San Joaquin Valley to a storage reservoir

formed by the San Luis Dam. The manmade lake at San Luis, with a capacity of more than two million acre-feet of water, makes possible the irrigation of 500,000 acres of rich but arid agricultural land in the lower San Joaquin Valley.

The installations already described, huge and costly as they are, are but part of the herculean task of storing the abundant water that falls on northern California and delivering the surplus to thirsty metropolitan and farming regions elsewhere in the state. Another part of the overall plan, which is financed jointly by state and federal funds, was the building of a third major dam, powerhouse, and reservoir, this one on the upper San Joaquin River. Part of the water stored there is fed into a canal and used to irrigate farmlands lying in the Madera area; the remainder of the water enters the Friant-Kern Canal and flows to the south, serving growers of grapes, citrus fruit, and other farm products as far away as Bakersfield, a distance of well over one hundred miles.

The Oroville Dam, which impounds the waters of the Feather River, is the cornerstone of the plan to "correct nature's oversight" by conserving part of northern California's superfluous water and delivering it to the southern end of the state. Work on this project began in 1961 and is scheduled for completion in the early 1970's. Once the system is in full operation, Feather River water will flow—at the rate of 1.8 million gallons per minute—down the east side of the valley, over the Tehachapi Mountains, and on southward almost to the Mexican border, a distance of 650 miles. During the crossing of the Tehachapis, a series of pumping stations will lift the water nearly two thousand feet above the valley floor.

From there it will flow by gravity into great storage reservoirs, and thence via a network of aqueducts and pipelines to its final destination in the homes and fields and factories of the southland.

While the main purpose of California's vast water-conservation program has been to bring water to those parts of the state that lack an adequate supply from other sources, that is by no means its only function. One of the many benefits it confers on residents of the nation's most populous state has already been mentioned; namely, the generation of electrical power, some of which is used to operate the pumping stations at Tracy and elsewhere, the balance being sold to communities through which the transmission lines pass. Revenue from that source, together with the fees paid by users of water for irrigation and other purposes, is expected ultimately to pay the entire cost of the project.

Moreover, the building of dams across the rivers has all but eliminated a hazard to which residents of the valley have been exposed for well over a century: that of having their lives endangered and their homes and crops threatened by periodic floods. For the immense quantities of water that flowed down to the lowlands each winter and spring, changing the rivers into roaring torrents and spreading over thousands of acres, now empties into manmade lakes, where it is stored, ready to be released as needed during the rainless months of summer and fall.

During the annual "dry" season the water is put to a variety of beneficial uses: to irrigate thousands of acres of farms and orchards and vineyards that are among the most productive in the nation; to provide a dependable year-around supply to cities and towns and industrial plants; and finally, to keep the water level in the Sacramento and San Joaquin rivers high enough to permit oceangoing steamers to ascend both rivers and carry the products of the valley to the markets of the world. When to these are added such incidental benefits as the preservation of wildlife and the facilities for recreation provided by the manmade lakes, the true significance of the valley's mighty water-control program becomes evident.

Index

88

ABOUT THE AUTHOR: Oscar Lewis, a prolific writer of adult and juvenile books as well as magazine articles, is the well-known historian of California and the Far West. Born and raised in San Francisco, Mr. Lewis and his wife make their home there. *The Sacramento River* is his first book for the Holt juvenile list.

ABOUT THE ARTIST: Michael Hampshire combines his talent as an illustrator with his enthusiasm for travel. He spent a month exploring the environs of the Sacramento River and collecting material for this book. Mr. Hampshire was born in Yorkshire, England, and studied at the University of Leeds before making New York City his home base.

ABOUT THE BOOK: The text is set in Janson and the display type is Craw Modern Bold. Michael Hampshire captures the history of the Sacramento River with dramatic pencil drawings that vary from bold line to soft shading.